Birds of Paradise

Winged Wonders

By Cyndy Unwin

Nature's CHILDREN

Children's Press®

An Imprint of Scholastic Inc.

Content Consultant
Katrina McCauley
Assistant Curator, Australia and the Islands
Columbus Zoo and Aquarium

Library of Congress Cataloging-in-Publication Data
Names: Unwin, Cynthia, author.
Title: Birds of paradise: winged wonders/by Cyndy Unwin.
Description: New York, NY: Children's Press, an imprint of Scholastic Inc., 2020. | Series: Nature's children | Includes index.
Identifiers: LCCN 2019004827| ISBN 9780531229897 (library binding) | ISBN 9780531239117 (paperback)
Subjects: LCSH: Birds of paradise (Birds)—Juvenile literature.
Classification: LCC QL696.P26 U59 2020 | DDC 598.8/65—dc23

Design by Anna Tunick Tabachnik

Creative Direction: Judith E. Christ for Scholastic Inc.

Produced by Spooky Cheetah Press

Printed in Heshan, China 62

SCHOLASTIC, CHILDREN'S PRESS, NATURE'S CHILDREN™, and associated logos
are trademarks and/or registered trademarks of Scholastic Inc.

1 2 3 4 5 6 7 8 9 10 R 29 28 27 26 25 24 23 22 21 20

Scholastic Inc., 557 Broadway, New York, NY 10012.

Photographs ©: cover: Tim Laman/National Geographic Creative; 1: Tim Laman/Getty Images; 4 top: Jim McMahon/Mapman®;
4 leaf silo and throughout: stockgraphicdesigns.com; 5 child silo: Nowik Sylwia/Shutterstock; 5 bird illustrations: Raichu/
Shutterstock; 5 bottom: Chien Lee/Minden Pictures; 6 bird silo and throughout: Artur Balytskyi/Shutterstock; 7: Tim Laman/The
National Geographic Image Collection/Nature Picture Library; 8: Tim Laman/Getty Images; 10-11: David Tipling Photo Library/
Alamy Images; 12-13: Otto Plantema/Buiten-beeld/Minden Pictures; 15: Giordano Cipriani/Getty Images; 16-17: Tim Laman/
Getty Images; 18-19: Tim Laman/Getty Images; 20-21: Tim Laman/Getty Images; 23: Tim Laman/Getty Images; 24 top left: Tim
Laman/National Geographic Creative; 24 top right: Tim Laman/Getty Images; 24 bottom left: Tim Laman/Getty Images;
24 bottom right: Tim Laman/Getty Images; 26-27: Tim Laman/The National Geographic Image Collection; 28-29: Tim Laman/
Getty Images; 30-31: Tim Laman/Getty Images; 33: The History Collection/Alamy Images; 34-35: ZSSD/Minden Pictures;
37: Natural History Museum, London, UK/Bridgeman Images; 38-39: David Tipling/FLPA/Minden Pictures; 40-41: Tim Laman/
Nature Picture Library; 42 left: Eric Isselee/Shutterstock; 42 right: Super Prin/Shutterstock; 43 left: clarst5/Shutterstock;
43 center: khlungcenter/Shutterstock; 43 right: Tim Laman/National Geographic Creative; 46: Tim Laman/National
Geographic Creative.

◀ **Cover image shows
a lesser bird of
paradise displaying.**

Table of Contents

Fact File: Birds of Paradise

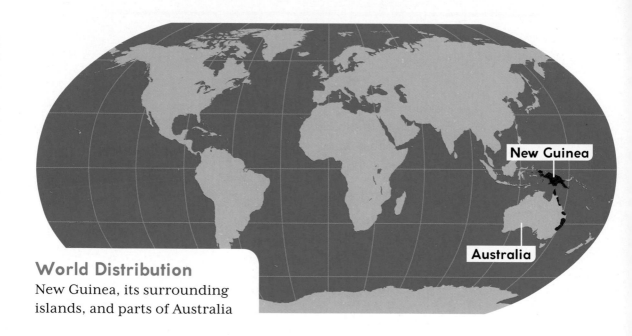

New Guinea

Australia

World Distribution
New Guinea, its surrounding islands, and parts of Australia

Habitat
Mostly forests, at various levels of the tree canopy; including rain forests, swamps, coastal mangroves, and subtropical forests

Habits
Nonmigratory; males engage in complex courtship displays; most females raise their young alone

Diet
Fruits, nuts, and seeds; arthropods and small vertebrates

Distinctive Features
Males of most species have elaborate plumage and vivid colors

Fast Fact
Most birds of paradise are solitary tree dwellers.

Size Range

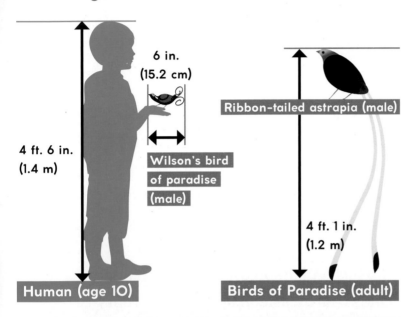

6 in.
(15.2 cm)

Wilson's bird
of paradise
(male)

4 ft. 6 in.
(1.4 m)

Human (age 10)

Ribbon-tailed astrapia (male)

4 ft. 1 in.
(1.2 m)

Birds of Paradise (adult)

◀ The standardwing
bird of paradise has
a crest at the top of
its beak.

5

CHAPTER 1

Beautiful Birds

Fog hangs low in the rain forest valley as the day begins. High above in the mountains, a bird with **plumes** the color of sunshine flutters among the trees. It lands on an open branch, showing off its bright feathers. The bird fluffs its long golden plumes up over its back, dances up and down the branch, and calls out loudly. *Wauk! Wauk! Wauk!* A plain brown bird, a female of the same species, lands nearby. The male's feather frenzy intensifies. This male show-off is hoping to be chosen as this female's **mate**.

There are more than 40 **species** of birds of paradise, and they are some of the most unusual animals on the planet. Each species is highly distinct. But most birds of paradise share two characteristics: The males tend to have eye-catching **plumage**, and they perform complex **courtship** rituals.

▶ A greater bird of paradise searches for a mate high in the canopy.

Vivid Colors attract females' attention.

Strong Beak pries apart fruit, nuts, and seeds.

Wiry Tail feathers wave during the male's courtship dance.

Colorful Wings add to the male's display.

Claws firmly grip tree branches.

Variety Is the Spice of Life

Birds of paradise come in a variety of sizes. The Wilson's bird of paradise is one of the smallest species. It could fit in your hand. The longest species is the ribbon-tailed astrapia. From the tip of his beak to the end of his tail feathers, the male is about as long as you are tall!

With some animals, like dogs and cats, the males and females in a species look alike. That is true for some birds, too. But not birds of paradise. Most males are quite distinct from the females of their species. Their bodies are about the same size. However, males tend to have intense colors and they may have specialized feathers. Female birds of paradise are usually brown or tan. Their only decoration may be stripes, bars, or contrasting colors on their heads, necks, and chests. Scientists think less-colorful feathers may provide **camouflage** for the females. This is especially important when they are nesting and raising their young.

◄ **This male king bird of paradise sports every color in the rainbow!**

Funky Feathers

In the bird world, feathers are a key to survival. Feathers help birds fly and keep them warm and cool. They also provide camouflage from **predators**. Bird of paradise feathers do all these things and more.

Many males actually have specialized feathers that help them attract mates. Several species have fluffy, wispy feathers that emerge just above their tail feathers. They are called plumes. Other male birds of paradise have feathers that look like wires. The twelve-wired bird of paradise has a dozen wire feathers curling away from its tail! Wires can come out from the birds' heads or from behind their wings, too. Some wires have tabs on the ends that look like flags.

Birds of paradise can also arrange their feathers into shapes that look like other things. When some males spread out their specialized feathers, they can make fans, capes, or even skirts!

▶ Can you guess how the twelve-wired bird of paradise got its name?

In Living Color

Many male birds of paradise also have vivid colors. These are important in attracting females. Some bird of paradise feathers have saturated colors (like dye). These feathers look the same from every direction. Other feathers are **iridescent**. The colors change depending on how the light hits them or from which angle they are viewed. Birds of paradise even have different kinds of black feathers. Some black feathers are shiny, and others are more like velvet. These velvety feathers are usually next to brighter or iridescent colors. The velvety black is *so* black that the colors beside them stand out more.

Birds of paradise have other colorful parts of their bodies, too. The Wilson's bird of paradise has purple feet and a "bald" head with bright blue skin. If you're lucky enough to glimpse a bird of paradise with its beak open, you might also see some interesting colors inside its mouth!

◀ This Wilson's bird of paradise has colorful feathers *and* colorful skin.

CHAPTER 2

Birds in Paradise

All birds of paradise live in one small area of the world. They are found in New Guinea, on its surrounding islands, and in a few parts of Australia. Most species live in the mountains, but their **habitats** can be very different. Some species live in the low rain forests or swamp forests near the ocean. Those birds are mostly **solitary**. Others live in the higher mountains. They tend to gather in groups.

Birds of paradise don't **migrate** as the seasons change. The climate where they live is bird-friendly. Even the cooler mountain habitats never get so cold that the birds' food supply runs out.

Many other types of birds fly long distances to find food or avoid harsh winters. Their bodies and feathers **evolved** for fast, efficient flying. Because birds of paradise are nonmigratory, the opposite is true for them. Their feathers may actually slow them down!

▶ New Guinea offers many habitats for birds of paradise.

Let's Eat ... Anything!

Birds of paradise are **omnivorous**. They can eat plants, insects, and spiders. They may also nibble on crustaceans, reptiles, small **vertebrates** such as frogs, and even baby birds. Food in their habitat is plentiful because there is little competition from other animals. Monkeys and apes don't live in this part of the world, so the birds don't have to share their fruit. And there are no squirrels gobbling up the nuts and seeds!

Even though birds of paradise can eat a variety of foods, most species are **frugivorous**. Fruit is a main part of their diet. Manucode birds of paradise love figs. For others, berries from the schefflera plant are their favorite food. The birds can't digest the seeds inside the berries, so they **regurgitate** them some distance away from the parent tree. That gives those seeds a chance to grow into new trees. When two species of plants or animals help each other out like this, it's called mutualism.

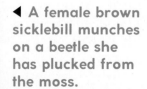
◀ A female brown sicklebill munches on a beetle she has plucked from the moss.

Mind Your Manners

Birds of paradise have many different feeding strategies. Their strong claws help them **perch** while they eat. But that's not all they can do! Just as you might use your hands to eat a slice of pizza, these birds can use their claws to hold on to their food. And all birds of paradise have strong beaks. Their beaks help them crack open the tough shells of nuts. They can also peck at insects inside thick moss and tree bark.

Many species, like the sicklebills, have sharp, curved beaks. They poke through the hard outer coverings of fruit **capsules** and dig out the juicy flesh of the fruit inside. These species can also use their beaks to sip nectar. Many birds of paradise are acrobatic eaters. They will dangle upside down from a tree branch if that's the only way to reach a delicious berry nearby!

▶ **This paradise riflebird has no problem dining upside down!**

Fast Fact
Ocean volcanoes
and earthquakes
formed New Guinea
and nearby islands.

Living the Good Life

The part of the world where birds of paradise live is **isolated**. New Guinea and its surrounding islands developed separately from the land masses nearby (including Asia). So the animal life in New Guinea is highly unusual. Just as there are no animals competing with birds of paradise for food, there are also no large predators for the birds to worry about. And that's a good thing—the males' vivid colors and fancy feathers would be easy to spot! Some males' feathers can also make a quick getaway difficult. The ribbon-tailed astrapia's tail feathers can be 3 feet (0.91 meters) long. Sometimes these long, flowing feathers get tangled in nearby branches. Then the bird has to use its beak to straighten out its tail before taking off!

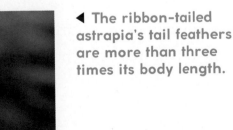

◀ The ribbon-tailed astrapia's tail feathers are more than three times its body length.

CHAPTER 3

The Greatest Show on Earth

So, it turns out that males' feathers

really *are* simply all for show! Males with the most impressive plumage have the best chance of mating with the most females. It's as simple as that!

By the time female birds are about one, they are looking for a mate. They look for the male with the best plumage and the most impressive courtship displays. This ensures that the best genes are passed on to the next generation.

The location of a male's display is called a court. For some, it's on a branch high in the trees. The males there display in a group called a lek. Other males make a solitary court on the forest floor. Wilson's, magnificent riflebird, and parotia birds of paradise clear a patch of ground until it is bare. Then they pluck leaves from the trees above to let sunlight through. This makes a "spotlight" on their court.

▶ A western parotia does a courtship dance for two females.

Red Bird of Paradise

▶ This male's curlicue tail wires are actually feathers!

Magnificent Riflebird

▶ It almost looks as if the female riflebird is dancing with the male.

Blue Bird of Paradise

▶ The male blue bird of paradise uses acrobatics to attract females.

Superb Bird of Paradise

▶ After forming his "face," this bird hops and dances along the branch.

Watch My Moves!

Male birds of paradise have different courtship displays. However, most use some combination of movement, positioning of their feathers, and color.

The red bird of paradise swings his body back and forth while he dances along a branch. His two tail wires sway to the beat as he spreads his wings wide, flapping and fluttering. Throughout the dance, the bird calls out loudly to any females that might be nearby.

The magnificent riflebird approaches a female and raises his wings like a vampire's cape. He snaps his head from side to side, showing off the colors on his neck.

The male blue bird of paradise dangles upside down below a female. He fans out his tail plumes and wires and makes them vibrate.

The superb bird of paradise looks like an alien! He tilts his head back and raises his cape to form a background for his iridescent breast shield. Two other spots of colorful feathers become the "eyes" of the alien.

◀ Male birds of paradise have lots of different dance moves!

Make Some Noise

Birds of paradise are famous for their feathers and colors. But it's not just looks that matter. The birds' **vocalizations** are just as interesting. Male birds use calls to announce their **territory**, advertise their presence to nearby females, and put on their courtship display. They might click, squawk, whistle, shriek, or even hiss. The brown sicklebill's call resembles a burst of gunfire. The bronze parotia sounds like a squeaker toy!

Goldie's bird of paradise males perform duets, singing together as they try to win a mate. At first they call out separately. Their calls merge into one sound as they approach the female. The duet ends mysteriously but politely. One male stays and the other quietly retreats.

Birds of paradise can also communicate in other ways. Males add sounds to their courtship rituals by beating their wings, snapping their specialized feathers, and rattling their bills.

▶ Which of these Goldie's birds of paradise will decide to step aside?

Fast Fact
Some of these birds put snake skins on their nests to deter predators.

Babes in Paradise

After mating, females in most species make cup nests in tree forks. They may use orchid tendrils, vines, twigs, leaves, and moss. The males usually play no part in nest building or chick **rearing**. The female lays one or two eggs and **incubates** them for two to four weeks, depending on the species.

After the chicks hatch, their eyes open in about six days. Their feathers appear just a few days later. This is usually the only time birds of paradise are in danger from predators. The chicks are small enough to be eaten by hawks and snakes. The chicks leave the nest at 20 to 30 days old. Sometimes, though, they stay with their mothers and continue to be fed by them for many weeks.

A few species of birds of paradise have different parenting behaviors from the others. For example, male and female manucode birds of paradise parent together. They usually raise two chicks. Another unique quality of these birds is that the males look similar to the females.

◀ These curl-crested manucode babies are ready to eat!

Learning the Moves

Male birds of paradise are ready to mate when they are two to four years old. (It depends on the species.) Every year, the birds **molt** their old feathers. The new feathers that grow in look a bit more mature. Still, it can take four to seven years for a male to grow his full adult plumage. Until then, the males look similar to the females of their species. Because of this, the young males can hang around more mature males. This gives them a chance to imitate their elders and practice their courtship behaviors. Because these rookies look like females, the older males don't see them as competition. They allow them to stay. The young males do attempt courtship displays. They try their best to win the attention of the females. But if there are more experienced and impressive males nearby, the females ignore the awkward tries of the youngsters.

▶ **A young male paradise riflebird practices his display.**

CHAPTER 4

Island Isolation

About 40 million years ago, a group of corvids began to evolve near New Guinea. These were the earliest **ancestors** of all crowlike birds, including birds of paradise. About 34 million years ago, many islands appeared out of the ocean. Scientists think some of these birds spread to the nearby continent of Asia by using the islands as "stepping stones." It is thought these birds evolved into common crows, ravens, and jays.

Eventually New Guinea became more isolated. The bird species in the area no longer crossed to the mainland. They began to develop their unique characteristics. About 20 million years ago, the corvids that would eventually evolve into the birds of paradise arose. It is thought these early birds of paradise may have resembled the current-day paradise-crow.

▶ This painting of a paradise-crow shows what early birds of paradise might have looked like.

Caw, Caw!

The closest relative of birds of paradise is the crow. The two bird families share many of the same features: strong claws and beaks, similar body shapes, loud calls, and omnivorous eating habits.

Crows don't have the colors and plumes that birds of paradise do. But they are just as impressive in another way. Crows are some of the most intelligent animals in the world. These birds have been known to use their beaks to make hooked tools. They use them to get grubs out of tree trunks. They can also make "rakes" from stiff leaves. Only a few animal species make their own tools—and most of them are primates, like humans! Some crows even understand traffic lights—and use them to their own advantage. Some city-dwelling crows perch on power lines and wait for traffic lights to turn red. Then they drop walnuts into the road. When the lights turn green, cars run over the nuts and crack their shells. When the lights turn red again, the crows swoop down to eat the pickings!

◀ This crow is using a twig to "fish" for insects inside the tree branch.

CHAPTER 5

Birds of Legend

In 1522, Spanish sailors sailing near New Guinea were given a gift of two dead birds of paradise. Their feathers were preserved, but their legs had been cut off. The lovely plumes were soon in high demand for Western ladies' hats. Indonesians exported many thousands of legless bird skins to Europe.

For more than a century, Westerners believed birds of paradise didn't have any legs! Mysterious **legends** arose about these almost supernatural birds that couldn't land. Some said the birds floated up to drink dew from the clouds. Famous artists, such as the Dutch painter Rembrandt, drew and painted the birds without legs. Of course, we now know that birds of paradise do have legs—and feet. A bit of legend is preserved in their scientific family name, Paradisaeidae, which means "footless paradise bird."

▶ As late as the 18th century, artists still depicted birds of paradise without legs!

Good News and Bad News

Birds of paradise have been hunted for thousands of years. The **indigenous** people of New Guinea believed the birds brought prosperity and safety to their communities. They used bird of paradise feathers for decorations in their rituals and ceremonies. Then, during the 19th century, there was a peak in plume trade for Western women's hats. About 50,000 bird of paradise skins were exported each year. Luckily, exportation was banned in the 1920s. Today, the numbers of most species are strong.

Hunting of birds of paradise by indigenous people continues, but their targets are fully plumed adult males. Females will accept younger, less showy mates if older males are not available. That ensures ongoing generations of birds. In addition, many birds of paradise live in wild, remote areas, so their habitat is not yet in danger.

There is bad news, though. Several species, including the Goldie's bird of paradise and the blue bird of paradise, are at risk. Almost all birds of paradise need forests. Many New Guinea forests are threatened by **deforestation** due to logging, oil palm plantations, and large-scale mining.

◀ A performer wears a headdress with Raggiana plumes.

Preserving Paradise Birds

The future of birds of paradise depends on humans near and far. The island of New Guinea is divided between two countries. Papua New Guinea is in the east and Indonesia is in the west. Indonesia has large nature **reserves** and national parks that preserve the habitat of birds of paradise. In Papua New Guinea, there are few official nature reserves. However, some landowners and villages are setting aside protected areas for wildlife.

Others around the world help, too. Zoos such as the Cincinnati Zoo have breeding programs for birds of paradise. Individuals can also make a difference. Since 2003, Edwin Scholes, an **ornithologist** from Cornell University, and Tim Laman, a National Geographic photographer, have researched birds of paradise. They have built awareness and support through their Birds-of-Paradise Project, which shares their discoveries with people like you and me.

Many mysteries still remain about birds of paradise. If we work to keep their forest habitats safe, we can learn more about these amazing winged creatures.

▶ Scholes searches for his next bird of paradise to study.

Birds of Paradise Family Tree

Birds of paradise are perching birds that live in trees. They are warm-blooded animals that have feathers and can fly. They lay eggs, from which their babies are born. This diagram shows how birds of paradise are related to other birds. The closer together the animals are on the tree, the more similar they are.

Flycatchers
birds that dart out from their perch to catch insects in midair

Parrots
birds with vivid colors that can mimic human speech

Ancestor of all Birds

Note: Animal photos are not to scale.

**Crows,
Shrikes,
and Jays**
vocal, intelligent,
and adaptable birds
with strong beaks
and claws

**Robins,
Finches, and
Sparrows**
common songbirds
that live in many
parts of the world,
including the
United States

**Birds of
Paradise**
birds from
New Guinea and
Australia with showy
feathers, colors, and
courtship rituals

Words to Know

A .... **ancestors** *(ANN-ses-turz)* family members who lived long ago

C .... **camouflage** *(KAM-uh-flahzh)* a way of hiding by using coloring, pattern, or shape to blend into one's surroundings

capsules *(KAP-suhlz)* closed casings on plants with seeds inside

courtship *(KORT-ship)* the act of seeking a mate

D .... **deforestation** *(dee-for-iss-TAY-shun)* the removal or cutting down of forests

E .... **evolved** *(i-VAHLVD)* changed slowly and naturally over time

F .... **frugivorous** *(froo-JIV-ur-uhs)* feeding on fruit

H .... **habitats** *(HAB-i-tats)* the places where an animal or plant is usually found

I .... **incubates** *(ING-kyuh-bayts)* keeps eggs warm before they hatch

indigenous *(in-DI-juh-nuhs)* living naturally in a region

iridescent *(ir-uh-DE-suhnt)* rainbowlike color that changes as the angle of view changes

isolated *(EYE-suh-lay-tid)* far separate from other people or things

L .... **legends** *(LEJ-uhndz)* stories handed down from earlier times, often based on fact but not entirely true

M .... **mate** *(MAYT)* a male or female partner

migrate *(MYE-grayt)* to move to another area or climate at a particular time of year

molt *(MOHLT)* to lose old fur, feathers, shell, or skin so that new ones can grow

O .... **omnivorous** *(ahm-NIV-ur-uhs)* eating both plants and meat

ornithologist *(or-nuh-THAH-luh-jist)* a scientist who studies birds

P .... **perch** *(PURCH)* to rest on a bar or branch

plumage *(PLOO-mij)* a bird's feathers

plumes *(PLOOMZ)* long, fluffy feathers

predators *(PRED-uh-tuhrs)* animals that hunt other animals for food

R .... **rearing** *(REER-ing)* the care for and bringing up of young

regurgitate *(ri-GUR-ji-tate)* to bring food that has been swallowed back from the stomach into the mouth

reserves *(rih-ZERVZ)* protected places where hunting is not allowed and where animals can live and breed safely

S .... **solitary** *(SAH-li-ter-ee)* not requiring or without the companionship of others

species *(SPEE-sheez)* one of the groups into which animals and plants are divided; members of the same species can mate and have offspring

T .... **territory** *(TER-i-tor-ee)* an area that an animal or group of animals uses and defends

V .... **vertebrates** *(VUR-tu-brates)* any animals that have a backbone

vocalizations *(voh-kuh-luh-ZAY-shuhnz)* sounds made to communicate

Find Out More

BOOKS

- Hyman, Jeremy. *Bird Brains: The Wild & Wacky World of Birds*. Lake Forest, CA: MoonDance Press, 2017.

- Laman, Tim, and Edwin Scholes. *Birds of Paradise: Revealing the World's Most Extraordinary Birds*. Washington, D.C.: National Geographic, 2012.

- Lindeen, Mary. *Dancing Bees and Other Amazing Communicators* (Searchlight Books—Animal Superpowers). Minneapolis, MN: Lerner Books, 2017.

- Turner, Pamela S. *Crow Smarts: Inside the Brain of the World's Brightest Bird* (Scientists in the Field). New York: Houghton Mifflin Harcourt, 2016.

- Yolen, Jane, Heidi E.Y. Stemple, Adam Stemple, and Jason Stemple. *Fly with Me: A Celebration of Birds Through Pictures, Poems, and Stories*. Washington, D.C.: National Geographic Kids, 2018.

To find more books and resources about animals, visit:

scholastic.com

Index

Index (continued)

About the Author

Cyndy Unwin lives in the mountains of Virginia and admires all the birds in the woods around her. Her favorites are the tiny but brave chickadees and the barred owls who greet each other at dusk. Cyndy teaches reading and writes books for children of all ages.